Welcome to the Garden of Your Mind

"Cultivate the garden within"
~ Proverb

Pull Your Weeds

Your mind is a garden and you are the gardener. Weeds represent your fears. They are habits that could be keeping you from creating an amazing life for yourself. Pull your weeds by writing out any negative thoughts you may have. In doing this you begin to identify self-destructive thought patterns.

Under the umbrella of fear, there are many emotions such as anger and frustration. Instead of judging your emotions and labeling them as good or bad, use them as a guide. Your emotions act as a valuable tool, they let you know where your energy is. Once you know where your energy is, you have better control in directing it where you want it to go. Try to look at fears and unhealthy behaviors as just old, out-dated habits that you no longer want to direct your life. Although these habits may be unhealthy, over time they have become a part of you and your identity. This can make it difficult to let go of negative patterns that have been created. However, the concept of living an unfulfilled, joyless life can be even more difficult to consider. As you recognize your fears and take responsibility for them, you can start to release the hold they have on you. Fears no longer control you when you look them straight in the face and tell them that you're taking your power back.

Recognize your fears, honor them, set them free and move forward. Writing is a safe and powerful way to release what you're feeling inside. You could write, "I now release the need to feel _____," or "This _____ behavior no longer serves me anymore." It may be necessary to repeat this process many times. When doing any self-work, especially releasing old issues, try to be compassionate, loving and patient with yourself. Cheer yourself on! Be careful that you are not only pulling the part of the weed that's above ground. Like any weed, if you don't pull the root, it can grow right back. Try to get to the root of your fears, this way you begin to release self-destructive thought patterns for good.

Let this inspire you: With every healthy, uplifting thought and every positive emotion you have, "feel-good" chemicals are released in your body. Choose healthy and uplifting thoughts!

By pulling weeds you can make room for new, positive seeds to be planted. It's never too late to regrow a garden, just as in any moment you can begin anew. If anything is stopping you, it's you!

Examples of Weeds

Worry
Envy
Insecurity
Anger
Doubt
Scarcity
Resentment
Frustration
Blame

Plant Your Seeds

"Your subconscious mind is like a bed of soil that accepts any kind of seed, good or bad. Your thoughts are active, they are seeds." - Joseph Murphy

Plant positive seeds by affirming what you want to grow in your garden. Write out statements that describe how you want to think, feel and act. Allow your positive seeds to take root. Try not to dig up new positive roots by thinking negatively. Do your best at becoming a detached observer and watch your thoughts closely. This will take practice. As you go about your day noticing your thoughts, ask yourself, "What types of thoughts am I 'planting' into my subconscious mind? What do I want to change about my habitual self-talk?" Use writing and drawing as tools to help reprogram thoughts that no longer serve you.

For example, you could write, "I deserve ___," or "I now plant seeds of ___," or "I am thankful for ___." (It's powerful to be thankful in advance.) You can also use the blank pages in the journal to make mini vision boards by cutting out words and pictures from magazines. Inspire yourself by creating uplifting pages to which you can refer when you feel the need to raise your energy. Let this inspire you: The energy of positive thoughts and feelings creates more positive energy. This energy is not draining, it flows freely and nourishes you. Wouldn't it be great to create a habit of this "life-giving" energy? Think of the wonderful people and experiences that will be drawn to you. Every thought creates. Have fun being the creative being that you are! Know that you deserve the best.

Quiet your mind and check your "deserving radar." If it's low, this may be an important topic to write about and work on. Know that you deserve to have all the wonderful things you imagine for yourself. There is enough for you and everyone. All successful gardens are tended to. You can water and fertilize the garden of your mind by repeating your affirmations. As your thought patterns begin to change, so will your feelings and emotions. This will change your perception, your experiences, and ultimately your world.

Only you can tend to your garden, just as only you can create your own happiness. Make planting seeds fun so that you continue with this process and make it a healthy habit. Use your imagination; it's a powerful tool that you can call on any time to better your moment, your day, your life.

Examples of Seeds

Peace
Confidence
Happiness
Trust
Prosperity
Balance
Well Being
Ease
Joy

Your Intention

Your intention with this journal may change as you change,
but it's always a good idea to set an intention when starting anything in life.

I intend to:

_____

_____

_____

_____

_____

_____

_____

_____

_____

_____

_____

_____

_____

_____

_____

_____

_____

_____

_____

The start of your day is a great time to set an intention.
Affirm: "Today is a new day and I am a new me!"

Pull Your Weeds   *Plant Your Seeds*

_____

_____

_____

_____

_____

_____

_____

_____

_____

_____

_____

_____

_____

_____

_____

_____

_____

_____

_____

_____

_____

_____

_____

You'll find great quotes throughout the journal. I hope they will inspire you!

"A journey of 1000 miles begins with a single step."
- Lao Tzu

Be Creative

Use the blank pages throughout the journal for letting your creative juices flow.
Although ideas are given along the way for inspiration, you are encouraged to use
this space for whatever calls to you. Trust that inner guidance! It's your dearest friend.

I'll be giving my 2 cents now and then too!

Pull Your Weeds   *Plant Your Seeds*

_____
_____
_____
_____
_____
_____
_____
_____
_____
_____
_____
_____
_____
_____
_____
_____
_____
_____
_____
_____
_____
_____
_____

Know that at any moment you can begin again! Isn't that comforting to know?

"*Your work is to discover your world and then with all your heart give yourself to it.*"
-Buddha

Be Creative
(Leave behind all judgments, please)

Put on uplifting music, light a candle... create your safe and sacred creative space.

Did you know you can actually get more done, when you take time to journal and meditate? Yep, you may be surprised to find that you're actually more productive. Give it a try.

Pull Your Weeds　　　　　　　*Plant Your Seeds*

When you first wake up from sleeping, think to yourself, "I now create a blissful day for myself. I am thankful and blessed." If you have trouble remembering to do this, write it down, keep the words by your bed until it becomes habit. Over time it can become as routine as brushing your teeth.

_____

_____

_____

_____

_____

_____

_____

_____

_____

_____

_____

_____

_____

_____

_____

_____

_____

_____

_____

_____

_____

_____

_____

_____

_____

_____

_____

_____

_____

_____

"What we think, we become."
~ Buddha

Be Creative

Make your own affirmation card. Create it here and then copy it onto a card to carry with you. Use words that describe how you want to be, such as, "I am amazing and creative".

Pull Your Weeds   *Plant Your Seeds*

_____

_____

_____

_____

_____

_____

_____

_____

_____

_____

_____

_____

_____

_____

_____

_____

_____

_____

_____

_____

_____

_____

_____

And breathe...

"Show me your garden and I shall tell you what you are."
~ Alfred Austin

Be Creative
What are you thinking right now?
How would your thoughts look if they were an actual garden?

Pull Your Weeds   *Plant Your Seeds*

You are already perfect just as you are! This process is just to help you create an even more amazing life for yourself and rid yourself of any unhealthy habits.

_____
_____
_____
_____
_____
_____
_____
_____
_____
_____
_____
_____
_____
_____
_____
_____
_____
_____
_____
_____
_____
_____
_____
_____
_____
_____

"I guess a good gardener always starts as a good weeder."
-Amos Pettingill

Be Creative

If you're not sure what to write about try starting with the words,
"I don't know what to write about or what I want to express...".
See what comes as you write about the state you are in and what you are feeling.
It is the same with drawing, start with doodling and see where it leads.

Isn't it funny how things just start to flow when you let go?

Pull Your Weeds   *Plant Your Seeds*

_____

_____

_____

_____

_____

_____

_____

_____

_____

_____

_____

_____

_____

_____

_____

_____

_____

_____

_____

_____

_____

_____

Try not to allow weeds to grow over those beautiful flowers!

_____

_____

_____

_____

_____

_____

_____

_____

_____

_____

_____

_____

_____

_____

_____

_____

_____

_____

_____

_____

_____

_____

_____

_____

_____

_____

"Yesterday is already a dream and tomorrow is only a vision, but today well-lived makes every yesterday a dream of happiness and every tomorrow a vision of hope."
~ Sanskrit Proverb

Be Creative

If you were to give yourself a flower, what would it look like?

Pull Your Weeds   *Plant Your Seeds*

_____
_____
_____
_____
_____
_____
_____
_____
_____
_____
_____
_____
_____
_____
_____
_____
_____
_____
_____
_____
_____
_____
_____
_____

Affirm: "If it is to be... it is up to me!"

_____

_____

_____

_____

_____

_____

_____

_____

_____

_____

_____

_____

_____

_____

_____

_____

_____

_____

_____

_____

_____

_____

"Come forth into the light of things, let nature be your teacher."
-William Wordsworth

Be Creative

Nature is constantly re-creating itself. You are a part of this creative process of life. It is a gift! Use this space to express how this makes you feel.

Isn't natuRe amaZing!?

Pull Your Weeds   *Plant Your Seeds*

_____

_____

_____

_____

_____

_____

_____

_____

_____

_____

_____

_____

_____

_____

_____

_____

_____

_____

_____

_____

_____

_____

_____

If not now... then when?   Go for it!

_____

_____

_____

_____

_____

_____

_____

_____

_____

_____

_____

_____

_____

_____

_____

_____

_____

_____

_____

_____

_____

_____

_____

_____

"A healthy garden is a reflection of a healthy soul."
~ Unknown

Be Creative

Have fun planting positive seeds of light, love, peace, joy, laughter, ease, comfort, balance, health, prosperity, and happiness into the garden of your creative mind!

Pull Your Weeds   *Plant Your Seeds*

_____

_____

_____

_____

_____

_____

_____

_____

_____

_____

_____

_____

_____

_____

_____

_____

_____

_____

_____

_____

_____

_____

Remember this one: "If at first you don't succeed then try and try again...".

_"The Universe is one great kindergarten for man.
Everything that exists has brought with it its own peculiar lesson."_

-Orison Swett Marden

Be Creative

Think of the times in your life when you have felt disappointed, only to find out that there was something better down the road. The time to have the most faith is when we can't see the whole picture. Difficult times can be a blessing in disguise.
Look for the lessons, keep faith and continue forward.

Feel overwhelmed sometimes? Breathe and just take the next step, you'll get there, slow and steady.

Pull Your Weeds   Plant Your Seeds

_____

_____

_____

_____

_____

_____

_____

_____

_____

_____

_____

_____

_____

_____

_____

_____

_____

_____

Write deeply... heal deeply.

"Take care of your garden and keep out the weeds,
fill it with sunshine, kind words and kind deeds."

~ Henry Longfellow

Be Creative

Use the top part of the page to draw or write what calls to you. Then sit comfortably, close your eyes and be still. Try to quiet your mind and let thoughts pass like clouds in the sky; practice detachment. Sit in this relaxed state for 5-10 minutes, then draw or write again on the bottom part of the page. Notice any difference between the 2 drawings and how you felt. Did you feel a shift in your energy and your expression?

Pull Your Weeds   *Plant Your Seeds*

_____

_____

_____

_____

_____

_____

_____

_____

_____

_____

_____

_____

_____

_____

_____

_____

_____

_____

_____

_____

_____

Don't wait for a reason to celebrate... every day is a good day!

"If you would be happy in your life, plant a garden."
~ Chinese Proverb

Be Creative

Choose happiness!
Create the happiest garden of your dreams.

🐞 ...

You know you don't have to wait until you see a ladybug, a falling star or a birthday candle to make a wish. Every moment is special enough to make a wish! How about making one now?

Pull Your Weeds   *Plant Your Seeds*

_____

_____

_____

_____

_____

_____

_____

_____

_____

_____

_____

_____

_____

_____

_____

_____

_____

_____

_____

_____

_____

_____

Imagination is a powerful tool, one you can access at any moment!

"To see things in the seed, that is genius."

~ Lao-Tzu

Be Creative

*What do you want your tomorrows to look like? Use your imagination!
If you start to question yourself STOP and remind yourself that doubt is
merely a thought, a thought that you have the power to change.*

Pull Your Weeds   *Plant Your Seeds*

_____

_____

_____

_____

_____

_____

_____

_____

_____

_____

_____

_____

_____

_____

_____

_____

_____

_____

_____

_____

_____

_____

_____

_____

Your thoughts create your experiences.
What kind of thoughts have you been thinking lately?

_____

_____

_____

_____

_____

_____

_____

_____

_____

_____

_____

_____

_____

_____

_____

_____

_____

_____

_____

_____

_____

_____

""The world always looks brighter from behind a smile."
- Anonymous

Be Creative

The mere act of smiling can release "feel-good" chemicals into your body.
Smile, laugh and have fun being creative!

Pull Your Weeds   *Plant Your Seeds*

_____

_____

_____

_____

_____

_____

_____

_____

_____

_____

_____

_____

_____

_____

_____

_____

_____

_____

_____

_____

_____

_____

_____

_____

_____

Affirm: "I create a life filled with calm and ease."

"A garden is a friend you can visit anytime."
~ Unknown

Be Creative

Learn how to be your own best friend.
Pretend you have a friend who is going through a tough time.
What would you draw and write for them to help lift their spirits?

Refer back to this page when you are feeling down, this is for you... your best friend!

Pull Your Weeds   *Plant Your Seeds*

_____

_____

_____

_____

_____

_____

_____

_____

_____

_____

_____

_____

_____

_____

_____

_____

_____

_____

_____

_____

_____

_____

_____

_____

You can perceive your life to be however you want it to be!
You know you deserve the best. Right?

_____

_____

_____

_____

_____

_____

_____

_____

_____

_____

_____

_____

_____

_____

_____

_____

_____

_____

_____

_____

_____

_____

_____

_____

_____

*"The comfortable and comforting people are those who look upon the bright side of life;
gathering its roses and sunshine and making the most that happens seem the best."*

~ Dorothy Dix

Be Creative

What does a peaceful day look like to you? Imagine what it feels like.
You can create peaceful days for yourself anytime you choose. It just takes practice.
Your imagination is like a muscle, the more you use it the stronger it gets.

Your imagination is free and open all day!

Pull Your Weeds   *Plant Your Seeds*

_____

_____

_____

_____

_____

_____

_____

_____

_____

_____

_____

_____

_____

_____

_____

_____

_____

_____

_____

_____

_____

_____

_____

You are more blessed than you know! Have you made a list of all the
things for which you are grateful? This is a good habit to get into!

"The thankful receiver bears a plentiful harvest."
~ William Blake

Be Creative

*Use this space to draw and write about the things for which you are thankful.
You can also use magazine clippings or whatever calls to you.*

🐞 ...

I'm thankful to be a part of this journey with you! You are a "wonder-full" being!

Pull Your Weeds   *Plant Your Seeds*

_____
_____
_____
_____
_____
_____
_____
_____
_____
_____
_____
_____
_____
_____
_____
_____
_____
_____
_____
_____
_____
_____
_____
_____
_____

La la la la la... dream a little dream... (or a big dream perhaps)!

"All the flowers of all the tomorrows are in the seeds of today."
~ Indian Proverb

Be Creative

Draw the garden of your dreams and then attach to each flower the thought it's having.
Like in a cartoon, use a balloon to encase its thought.

_____

_____

_____

_____

_____

_____

_____

_____

_____

_____

_____

_____

_____

_____

_____

_____

_____

_____

_____

_____

_____

_____

_____

_____

_____

_____

Pull Your Weeds   *Plant Your Seeds*

_____

_____

_____

_____

_____

_____

_____

_____

_____

_____

_____

_____

_____

_____

_____

_____

_____

_____

_____

_____

_____

_____

Ready to correct out-dated thoughts and change your mind?

"Trees are the earth's endless effort to speak to the listening heaven."
-Rabindranath Tagore

Be Creative

(Leave behind all judgments please.)

Stand up and stretch; raise your arms in the air and stretch out your fingers; next bend over and reach to your toes; then slowly raise your arms to the sky once more. Notice how just this simple stretch can affect your body, mind and spirit. Now see what comes to you ...

Pull Your Weeds   *Plant Your Seeds*

_____

_____

_____

_____

_____

_____

_____

_____

_____

_____

_____

_____

_____

_____

_____

_____

_____

_____

_____

_____

_____

_____

_____

_____

_____

Oh happy day!

_____

_____

_____

_____

_____

_____

_____

_____

_____

_____

_____

_____

_____

_____

_____

_____

_____

_____

_____

_____

_____

_____

_____

"He who plants a garden, plants happiness."
~ Chinese Proverb

Be Creative

Draw and write about things in your life that make you happy, light, and free.

Happy, happy, joy, joy!

Pull Your Weeds   *Plant Your Seeds*

_____

_____

_____

_____

_____

_____

_____

_____

_____

_____

_____

_____

_____

_____

_____

_____

_____

_____

_____

_____

_____

_____

_____

Trust and let go... trust and let grow!

_____

_____

_____

_____

_____

_____

_____

_____

_____

_____

_____

_____

_____

_____

_____

_____

_____

_____

_____

_____

_____

_____

_____

_____

_____

"Self-trust is the first secret of success."
~ Ralph Waldo Emerson

Be Creative

Trust the process of life.
You can let go and start anew ... just as you are able to re-grow a whole garden any time.

Create a mantra that's just for you, to call on in any moment. Make it a catchy phrase so you'll always remember it. Mine is, "I am healthy, I am strong, I have energy all day long!"

Pull Your Weeds   *Plant Your Seeds*

Get clear about what you want, visualize it, feel it. Remember to... "act as if "!
Act as if you are confident, strong, and filled with peace (or whatever it is you're working on).

_____

_____

_____

_____

_____

_____

_____

_____

_____

_____

_____

_____

_____

_____

_____

_____

_____

_____

_____

_____

_____

_____

_____

_____

_____

_____

_____

"Gardening is a way of showing that you believe in tomorrow."
~ Unknown

Be Creative

*Here is a fun way to "act as if": Think of your life as your stage production,
your very own "play." You are the star, the director, the writer and the producer. You have
the power to rewrite your character and to act how you want your character to act.
While it takes practice and "rehearsals", as preparing for any role does... YOU CAN DO IT!*

...and action!

Pull Your Weeds   *Plant Your Seeds*

_____

_____

_____

_____

_____

_____

_____

_____

_____

_____

_____

_____

_____

_____

_____

_____

_____

_____

_____

_____

_____

_____

Sometimes, just a little effort is all it takes to shift your energy.

"One flower can wake the dream!"
~ Unknown

Be Creative

Start with one inspirational thought and/or drawing – see how that one leads to another and then another – notice how many new ideas enter your mind. Entertain the healthy, positive ideas and give a "no thanks" to any thoughts that aren't nurturing.

What you focus on expands!

Pull Your Weeds　　　　　　　*Plant Your Seeds*

_____

_____

_____

_____

_____

_____

_____

_____

_____

_____

_____

_____

_____

_____

_____

_____

_____

_____

_____

_____

_____

You're always changing! Right now and right now and right now and...
I think you get the picture. You cannot not change!

"In all things of nature there is something of the marvelous."

~ Aristotle

Be Creative

Use the nature of change to your advantage. Recognize how it's harder for things to change when you hold on too tight and how letting go allows everything to fall into place perfectly. It takes practice to let go. Encourage yourself along the way.

It feels good to let go! I carried that weight around long enough. Did my shoulders just drop 2 inches?

Pull Your Weeds   *Plant Your Seeds*

_____
_____
_____
_____
_____
_____
_____
_____
_____
_____
_____
_____
_____
_____
_____
_____
_____
_____
_____
_____
_____
_____
_____
_____
_____

Thinking negatively is just a habit.
Do you know what's great about habits? They can be broken!

"We are what we repeatedly do. Excellence, therefore, is not an act but a habit."

~ Aristotle

Be Creative

Make planting positive seeds a habit! Use this space to recognize some of your habits. Be honest with yourself during this process. Getting frustrated with yourself is a habit that can be broken and replaced with one of compassion and patience.

Pull Your Weeds   *Plant Your Seeds*

_____
_____
_____
_____
_____
_____
_____
_____
_____
_____
_____
_____
_____
_____
_____
_____
_____
_____
_____
_____
_____
_____
_____
_____
_____

Keep on keepin' on! I believe in you!

_____

_____

_____

_____

_____

_____

_____

_____

_____

_____

_____

_____

_____

_____

_____

_____

_____

_____

_____

_____

_____

_____

_____

_____

_____

_____

"More grows in the garden than the gardener sows."
~ Spanish Proverb

Be Creative

If you could have exactly the life you've imagined, what would it look like?
Don't sell yourself short... you can have it all!

Pull Your Weeds   *Plant Your Seeds*

_____

_____

_____

_____

_____

_____

_____

_____

_____

_____

_____

_____

_____

_____

_____

_____

_____

_____

_____

_____

_____

Affirm: "Today is a new day... and I am a new me!"

_____

_____

_____

_____

_____

_____

_____

_____

_____

_____

_____

_____

_____

_____

_____

_____

_____

_____

_____

_____

_____

_____

_____

_____

_____

_____

_____

"Adopt the pace of nature; her secret is patience."
~ Ralph Waldo Emerson

Be Creative

What weeds are lingering? Some may have a stronger hold and be rooted deeper than others. Draw pictures of these weeds and label them.

Pull Your Weeds   *Plant Your Seeds*

_____
_____
_____
_____
_____
_____
_____
_____
_____
_____
_____
_____
_____
_____
_____
_____
_____
_____
_____
_____
_____
_____
_____

Try and go the whole day without complaining once. Go three days
and then try a week. Could you go a whole month? I think you could!

"We can complain because rose bushes have thorns,
or rejoice because thorn bushes have roses."

~ Abraham Lincoln

Be Creative

As you change your thoughts your perceptions then change. Take a deep breath, look inside yourself and decide what perceptions you have that are or aren't working for you.

Want to know a trick to change other people? Change yourself and your perceptions.

Pull Your Weeds   *Plant Your Seeds*

_____

_____

_____

_____

_____

_____

_____

_____

_____

_____

_____

_____

_____

_____

_____

_____

_____

_____

_____

_____

_____

_____

Keep Going! Writing is an amazing and powerful way to transform energy!

"The thought manifests as the word; The word manifests as the deed;
The deed develops into habit; And habit hardens into character. So watch the thought and
its ways with care, and let it spring from love; Born out of concern for all beings."

~ Buddha

Be Creative

Ponder how your outside world is a reflection of your inside world.

Pull Your Weeds   *Plant Your Seeds*

_____

_____

_____

_____

_____

_____

_____

_____

_____

_____

_____

_____

_____

_____

_____

_____

_____

_____

_____

_____

_____

_____

_____

Spread your wings and fly butterfly... fly! You can do it!

_____

_____

_____

_____

_____

_____

_____

_____

_____

_____

_____

_____

_____

_____

_____

_____

_____

_____

_____

_____

_____

_____

_____

_____

_____

_____

"Just when the caterpillar thought the world was over, it became a butterfly."
~ Unknown

Be Creative

If you were a butterfly, what would you look like?
In what ways are you ready to spread your wings and fly?

Pull Your Weeds   *Plant Your Seeds*

_____

_____

_____

_____

_____

_____

_____

_____

_____

_____

_____

_____

_____

_____

_____

_____

_____

_____

_____

_____

_____

Everyone has to pull their own weeds. Even if you want to pull others for them, you can't. By pulling them, you wouldn't be honoring their journey. We each have our own life lessons. A good way to help others is by giving support, being compassionate and by being an example.

"Everyone has enough weeding to do in their own garden."
~ Flemish Proverb

Be Creative

*Have you been trying to fix others? Sometimes that can distract you from our own work.
We must each tend to our own gardens.*

In blessing others you bless yourself, in giving to others you give to yourself. Now that's magic!!

Pull Your Weeds　　　　　　　*Plant Your Seeds*

_____
_____
_____
_____
_____
_____
_____
_____
_____
_____
_____
_____
_____
_____
_____
_____
_____
_____
_____
_____
_____
_____
_____

Make a point to get outside every day and feel the sunshine on your face.
Is it cloudy out? Use your imagination to feel what a sunny day would be like.

"The flower that follows the sun does so even on cloudy days."
~ Robert Leighton

Be Creative

Use your imagination... create your sunny day.

I love the song "Good day sunshine", by the Beatles. You know I'm a beetle too!

Pull Your Weeds   *Plant Your Seeds*

_____

_____

_____

_____

_____

_____

_____

_____

_____

_____

_____

_____

_____

_____

_____

_____

_____

_____

_____

_____

_____

_____

_____

If you're unsure about something... try asking for guidance.
Affirm: "I am guided perfectly always and in all ways."

"*There is guidance for each of us, and by lowly listening we shall hear the right word.*"

~ *Ralph Waldo Emerson*

Be Creative

Get quiet, trust your guidance and see what comes to you.

🐞 ...

I felt guided to share this journey with you and look how great it has worked out!

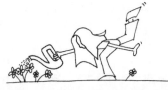

Pull Your Weeds   *Plant Your Seeds*

_____

_____

_____

_____

_____

_____

_____

_____

_____

_____

_____

_____

_____

_____

_____

_____

_____

_____

_____

_____

_____

_____

Pay attention to the miracles around you and keep a feeling of wondrous awe!

_____

_____

_____

_____

_____

_____

_____

_____

_____

_____

_____

_____

_____

_____

_____

_____

_____

_____

_____

_____

_____

_____

_____

_____

_____

_____

_____

"You yourself, as much as anybody in the entire universe,
deserve your love and affection."
~ Buddha

Be Creative

Call on your inner child.
Draw and write about some positive things from childhood that you remember.
Maybe it's a swing set or tree house, playing in the park or a family camping trip.
Did you spend a lot of time in nature? Have you been spending time in nature lately?
What's stopping you? What are the things that you love to do but keep putting off?

Lay on a blanket under a tree, look up at the sky and find fun creative shapes in the clouds.

Pull Your Weeds   *Plant Your Seeds*

_____

_____

_____

_____

_____

_____

_____

_____

_____

_____

_____

_____

_____

_____

_____

_____

_____

_____

_____

_____

_____

_____

_____

Have you listened lately to the music of nature?
Wind blowing, leaves rustling, birds chirping... for a garden it's the # 1 song of all time!

"Keep a green tree in your heart and perhaps a singing bird will come"
-Chinese Proverb

Be Creative

Quiet your mind and sit outside in nature somewhere. Feel the amazing energy
live plants exude. Allow your senses to take in all the sights and sounds.
Use this space to express your experience:

Pull Your Weeds   *Plant Your Seeds*

_____

_____

_____

_____

_____

_____

_____

_____

_____

_____

_____

_____

_____

_____

_____

_____

_____

_____

_____

_____

_____

_____

Speak words of kindness, compassion and encouragement to
yourself and others. We are all connected. We are all one.

_____

_____

_____

_____

_____

_____

_____

_____

_____

_____

_____

_____

_____

_____

_____

_____

_____

_____

_____

_____

_____

_____

_____

_____

_____

"Words have the power to both destroy and heal.
When words are both true and kind, they can change our world."
~ Buddha

Be Creative

It is not your responsibility to tend to the gardens of others.
We each find our own way at our own time, just as nature intended.
In what ways can you simply just be the example?

Pull Your Weeds   *Plant Your Seeds*

_____

_____

_____

_____

_____

_____

_____

_____

_____

_____

_____

_____

_____

_____

_____

_____

_____

_____

_____

_____

_____

_____

We really only have this moment, right now. "In-joy" your present (it truly is a gift)!

"The secret of health for both mind and body is not to mourn for the past, not to worry about the future, or not to anticipate troubles, but to live in the present moment wisely and earnestly."

~ Buddha

Be Creative

How does the garden of your mind change when you become present?
Notice how maybe the weeds seem to not have such a hold or be as
prevalent or how the flowers seem to be extra vibrant and abundant.

Pull Your Weeds   *Plant Your Seeds*

_____
_____
_____
_____
_____
_____
_____
_____
_____
_____
_____
_____
_____
_____
_____
_____
_____
_____
_____
_____
_____
_____
_____
_____
_____

Go back and read the intention you wrote at the beginning of the journal.
Notice how much you have changed since that time. What is your intention for today?

"All the flowers of all the tomorrows are in the seeds of today."
~ Indian Proverb

Be Creative

Put forth intentions of love, peace, light, joy, and laughter. Have the inner knowing that all is well. Pull this energy into your being by using the power of imagination. Now, have fun expressing yourself...

Know this... YOU ARE POWERFUL!

Pull Your Weeds   *Plant Your Seeds*

_____

_____

_____

_____

_____

_____

_____

_____

_____

_____

_____

_____

_____

_____

_____

_____

_____

_____

_____

_____

_____

_____

_____

No more excuses, it's time to take responsibility for your thoughts, words and actions.
You get to choose! What a liberating feeling!

_____
_____
_____
_____
_____
_____
_____
_____
_____
_____
_____
_____
_____
_____
_____
_____
_____
_____
_____
_____
_____
_____
_____
_____
_____
_____
_____

"Be like the flower, turn your faces to the sun."
-Kahlil Gibran

Be Creative

Have you seen evidence that your thoughts are creative?
What have you noticed today?

Pull Your Weeds   *Plant Your Seeds*

_____
_____
_____
_____
_____
_____
_____
_____
_____
_____
_____
_____
_____
_____
_____
_____
_____
_____
_____
_____
_____
_____
_____
_____
_____

As you learn more you grow more and as you grow more
you learn more, it's a beautiful dance of awakening!

"We are disturbed not by what happens to us, but by our thoughts about what happens."

- Epictetus

Be Creative

It's okay to be afraid. The important thing is to step through the fear.
Every time you allow fear to hold you back, you only give it more power over you.
In what ways can you dissolve your fears by changing you thinking?
What are you thinking now? How are those thoughts shaping your future?

Don't like how you've been thinking lately? You can always choose again.

Pull Your Weeds   *Plant Your Seeds*

_____
_____
_____
_____
_____
_____
_____
_____
_____
_____
_____
_____
_____
_____
_____
_____
_____
_____
_____
_____
_____
_____
_____
_____
_____

Let it grow, let it grow, let it grow.

"As the garden grows, so does the gardener."
~ Hebrew Proverb

Be Creative

In what ways have you grown since starting this journal?
How have you started to take responsibility for your weeds?

Pull Your Weeds   *Plant Your Seeds*

_____

_____

_____

_____

_____

_____

_____

_____

_____

_____

_____

_____

_____

_____

_____

_____

_____

_____

_____

_____

_____

_____

Let the light in your heart shine, let the wings of your spirit soar and
let the seeds of your mind blossom! You have it all right there... in you!

_____

_____

_____

_____

_____

_____

_____

_____

_____

_____

_____

_____

_____

_____

_____

_____

_____

_____

_____

_____

_____

_____

_____

_____

_____

_____

"Give me odorous at sunrise a garden of beautiful flowers where I can walk undisturbed."
~ Walt Whitman

Be Creative

Create a garden in your mind that you can visit any time, to find peace and solace.
Gift yourself with this.

This little light of mine, I'm gonna let it shine!

Pull Your Weeds   *Plant Your Seeds*

_____
_____
_____
_____
_____
_____
_____
_____
_____
_____
_____
_____
_____
_____
_____
_____
_____
_____
_____
_____
_____

I'm proud of you! Are you proud of yourself?

"I go to nature to be soothed and healed, and to have my senses put in order."
-John Burroughs

Be Creative

When worries come up, try not to keep them inside where they may build up. Use your journal to express what may be bothering you. Then go dance, sing a song, go for a walk or do some light stretches. After, come back and work with the journal more. Notice how your attitude has shifted and your thoughts and body have become lighter.

Worry is just another habit you can break. Work at watching your self-talk.

_____

_____

_____

_____

_____

_____

_____

_____

_____

_____

_____

_____

_____

_____

_____

_____

_____

_____

_____

_____

_____

_____

_____

Pull Your Weeds   *Plant Your Seeds*

_____

_____

_____

_____

_____

_____

_____

_____

_____

_____

_____

_____

_____

_____

_____

_____

_____

_____

_____

_____

_____

I hope you're making it a beautiful day for yourself!

"Hope is a waking dream."
-Aristotle

Be Creative

Share your hopes and dreams with the most important person in your life... you!

Pull Your Weeds   *Plant Your Seeds*

_____

_____

_____

_____

_____

_____

_____

_____

_____

_____

_____

_____

_____

_____

_____

_____

_____

_____

_____

_____

_____

_____

_____

Motivate yourself and become dedicated to creating the life you want. Be your own life-coach.

"The glory of gardening: hands in the dirt, head in the sun, heart with nature.
To nurture a garden is to feed not just on the body, but the soul."

-Alfred Austin

Be Creative

Have fun using your imagination!
Remember... like a muscle, the more you use it the stronger it becomes.

Let's go! Work those imagination muscles! You can do it, if you put your mind to it!

Pull Your Weeds   *Plant Your Seeds*

_____

_____

_____

_____

_____

_____

_____

_____

_____

_____

_____

_____

_____

_____

_____

_____

_____

_____

_____

_____

_____

_____

_____

Miracles are happening all around you!

"If we could see the miracle of a single flower clearly, our whole life would change."
~ Buddha

Be Creative

You are a miracle! Draw and write from this perspective...

I'm a miracle too, just like you!

Pull Your Weeds　　　　　　　　*Plant Your Seeds*

The past is in the past. Wow, that's cool!

"The appearance of things change according to the emotions, and thus we see magic and beauty in them, while the magic and beauty are really in ourselves."

~ Kahlil Gibran

Be Creative

Know the past has no power over you. Leave all judgments behind and have fun...

Pull Your Weeds   *Plant Your Seeds*

_____

_____

_____

_____

_____

_____

_____

_____

_____

_____

_____

_____

_____

_____

_____

_____

_____

_____

_____

_____

_____

_____

Honor yourself for who you are. Cherish the fact that you are a divine being!

"*Every blade of grass has its angel that bends over it and whispers, 'Grow, grow.'*"
~ The Talmud

Be Creative

What has this journey of self-discovery meant to you? How have you changed?
I hope you have found courage to release unhealthy habits, focus and discipline
to create healthy new habits, and compassion for yourself and for others.
Most importantly, I hope you have realized how truly amazing and powerful you are!

Life really is a gift, isn't it? "In-joy" your journey! I'll see you out there, in the garden of life!